# THE GLASS CASTLE

## Jeannette Walls

AUTHORED by Andrea Clay
UPDATED AND REVISED by Elizabeth Weinbloom

COVER DESIGN by Table XI Partners LLC
COVER PHOTO by Olivia Verma and © 2005 GradeSaver, LLC

BOOK DESIGN by Table XI Partners LLC

Published by GradeSaver LLC, www.gradesaver.com

First published in the United States of America by GradeSaver LLC. 2011

GRADESAVER, the GradeSaver logo and the phrase "Getting you the grade since 1999" are registered trademarks of GradeSaver, LLC

ISBN 978-1-60259-256-8

Printed in the United States of America

For other products and additional information please visit
http://www.gradesaver.com

# Table of Contents

# Table of Contents

# Biography of Walls, Jeannette (1960-)

Jeannette Walls was born on April 21, 1960 to Rex and Rose Mary Walls in Phoenix, Arizona. She is the Walls' third child; though at her birth Rex and Rosemary had already lost one daughter at only 9-months of age. As a child Jeannette was tall and skinny with red hair like her siblings Brian and Lori. Her first memory is being burned by a fire while cooking hot dogs at age three. Jeannette's memoir details the story of her life, which is characterized by constant movement and unconventional parents.

After her junior year of high school Jeannette moved away from home to live in New York City with her older sister, Lori. There she began her career as a journalist, working for *The Phoenix*. She graduated from Barnard College in 1984 with honors. Walls is known for her work on the MSNBC.com gossip column "Scoop". She is also the author of three books: *Dish: The Inside Story on the World of Gossip* (2000), *The Glass Castle* (2005), and her first fiction work *Half Broke Horses: A True-Life Novel* (2009), which details the life of her grandmother Lilly Smith.

In 1988 Walls was married to Eric Goldberg. The two later divorced and she was remarried to John Taylor, a fellow journalist, in 2002. Walls has contributed to *New York magazine*, *Esquire*,and *USA Today*. She has also been interviewed on the Oprah Winfrey Show and *The Today Show*. She currently lives in Virginia with her husband John Taylor and continues to contribute regularly to MSNBC.

# About The Glass Castle

Jeannette Walls' 2005 memoir *The Glass Castle* details the joys and struggles of her childhood. It offers a look into her life and that of her highly charismatic yet frequently dysfunctional family. Walls' first memoir and second non-fiction work, *The Glass Castle* was received well by critics and the public.

*The Glass Castle* remained on the *New York Times Bestseller's List* for 100 weeks and received The Christopher Award, the American Library Association's Alex Award and the *Books for Better Living Award*. In only two years the book had sold over 1.5 million copies and had been translated into six other languages. Paramount Pictures purchased the rights to produce a film based on the memoir but the project has yet to conclude.

In an article for "Publisher's Weekly" Walls wrote of her surprise that many thought her memoir was largely fictionalized and exaggerated. She contested the claims of some reviewers and readers, claiming that her work was based entirely on her memory. Truth, Walls says is "the most important goal of a memoir writer". But she also writes that truth varies based on the person telling it, memories she has growing up are recounted different by her other family members, "my brother, my sisters and my mother have all said that while they felt my book was substantially true, any memoir they would have written would have been entirely different".

# Character List

**Cindy Thompson**

A girl in Welch who tries to befriend Jeannette and convince her to join the junior Ku Klux Klan.

**The Grady Kids**

Twelve children who also lived on Hobart Street. The children had no father and their mother was bed-ridden. The boys lived uninhibited and wildly. Rose Mary said they were an example of people who were worse off than her own children.

**Kenny Hall**

A forty-two year old man with a mental disability. The children in Welch played tricks on him and told him that the could go on a date with Jeannette if he did something for them. Many Saturday nights Jeannette had to explain to a crying and complaining Kenny that she did not date older men and she would not go out with him.

**Ginnie Sue Pastor**

The "town whore" in Welch, Ginnie is thirty-three years old with 9 children. She is married to Clarence Pastor who has black lung.

**Clarence Pastor**

Ginnie Sue's husband. Clarence is plagued by black lung and spends his days sitting in his home.

**Kathy Pastor**

Ginnie's oldest daughter. Kathy is teased at school for being the daughter of a whore. Kathy befriends Jeannette and convinces her to come to her home to tell her mother about life in California.

**Sweet Man Pastor**

Ginnie's youngest son.

**Ernie Goad**

A kid in Welch who bullies Jeannette and Brian and calls their family garbage. Brian and Jeannette team up to fend off Ernie and his gang in an effort they later called the 'Battle of Little Hobart Street'.

**The Noes**

The Walls' neighbors on Little Hobart Street. Karen and Carol are the Noe girls.

### Tinkle

The family dog. A Jack Russel terrier who lives with them on Little Hobart Street.

### Iggy

The iguana that Brian picks up while the family is living in Welch because it reminds him of the desert. Iggy freezes to death one night because the Walls could not afford to heat their house that winter.

### Carrie Mae Blankenship

A classmate of Jeannette's in Welch. When Jeannette goes over to Carrie Mae's house she learns what a thermostat is and wishes that they had one in the house on Little Hobart Street to keep them warm during the winter.

### Lucy Jo Rose

A fellow teacher of Jeannette's at Davy elementary school. Lucy Jo is ordered by the principal to give Rose Mary a ride to the school since the Walls family was still without a car. Lucy Jo resents Rose Mary for this duty and treats Rose Mary as though she is a dirty person.

### Miss Jeannette Bivens

A teacher at Welch High School. Miss Bivens is Jeannette's faculty adviser for the school newspaper. She also was Rex's English teacher when he attended the school, and the teacher who convinced him to stay in school and get his diploma. Rex named Jeannette after this teacher.

### Robbie

A man who Rex bets in a bar playing pool. Robbie flirts with Jeannette and gets a little too aggressive which makes Jeannette resent her father for endangering her safety.

### Mr. Becker

The owner of Becker's Jewel Box. He hires Jeannette as an assistant and pays her $40 an hour.

### Ken Fink and Bob Gross

Two filmmakers who come from New York to Welch as part of a government cultural enrichment program. They encourage Lori to move to New York City if she is serious about becoming an artist.

### Oz

The name of the piggy bank that the Walls children use to collect funds for the escape out of Welch.

## The Sanders Family

Jeannette babysat for this family while living in Welch. When the family decides to move to Iowa they take Lori with them to work for the summer and promise to buy her a ticket to New York as compensation after the summer ends.

## Chuck Yeager

A native West Virginian, war hero, and aviation pioneer Chuck Yeager visits Welch high school to give a motivational speech. He is Rex's hero and Rex is very excited to hear that he is coming. Jeannette conducts an interview with him for the school newspaper.

## Evan

Lori's friend in New York. He picks up Jeannette from the train station when she arrives in New York City.

## Mike Armstrong

Owner, publisher and editor-in-chief of *The Phoenix*, a newspaper Jeannette interns with during her first summer in New York.

## Eric

Jeannette's first husband. Eric is from a wealthy family and company owner. He lives on Park Avenue and invites Jeannette to move in with him after she graduates from Barnard.

## Dinitia Hewitt

an African American classmate of Jeannette's in Welch. Dinitia and her followers bully Jeannette at Welch Elementary. The two later become friends after Dinitia witnesses Jeannette helping a neighbor escape a dog attack. Dinitia becomes pregnant in seventh grade and is arrested for stabbing her mother's boyfriend to death. It is implied that her mother's boyfriend sexually assaulted Dinitia.

## Miss Caparossi

Jeannette's teacher at Welch Elementary School. She accuses Jeannette for thinking that she is better than her and the other students in West Virginia.

## Professor Fuchs

Jeannette's professor at Barnard.She challenges Jeannette's views on the homeless and Jeannette is too ashamed to tell her that her opinions are informed by her own life.

## Uncle Stanley

Smells of whiskey and lives with his parents. He is extremely happy to meet the children of his brother and smothers them with hugs and kisses.

### Ted Walls

Rex's father. He speaks in a mumble and has short, white, hair.

### Erma Walls

Rex's mother who lives in West Virginia. She refuses to be called 'Grandma' because it makes her feel old. Erma has a grumpy disposition and asks her grandchildren to refrain from laughing in her home.

### Mrs. Ellis

Jeannette's fourth grade teacher in Phoenix

### Edward

the name the children give to Rose Mary's wooden mannequin which she used for her artwork.

### Miss Shaw

Jeannette's third grade teacher in Phoenix. She moves Jeannette to a gifted reading group.

### Bertha Whitefoot

a half-indian woman and neighbor of the Walls in Battle Mountain. Her yard is full of dogs and enclosed by a fence. She calls Billy Deel "the devil with a crew cut".

### Grandma Smith (Lilly Smith)

Rose Mary's mother and a former teacher. She is the opposite of her daughter and is very particular about how things should be done. Grandma Smith's strictness is partly to blame for Rose Mary's lenient and flexible parent style. Throughout their travels the Walls family would sometimes stay in Grandma Smith's house in Phoenix.

### Jim

Rose Mary's brother.

### Billy Deel

Billy moves to Battle Mountain when Jeannette is eight and he is eleven. He lives with his father in a house close to the Walls' home. He is tall and skinny with blue eyes and an uneven head.

**Ginger**

a prostitute who lives in the Green Lantern. Rex brings her to dinner with him and Brian on Brian's birthday.

**Buster**

a wounded Buzzard that Rex brings home to the family in Battle Mountain to live with them. The bird is grumpy and refuses food and Jeannette is glad when he finally heals and flies away.

**Carla**

Jeannette's friend in Battle Mountain. Jeannette scrapes her thigh at Carla's house but Rose Mary refuses to take Jeannette to the hospital, remarking that people were too quick to go to the doctor even after only a minor injury.

**Miss Page**

Jeannette's second grade teacher who is prone to anger and violent outbreaks. She is fired when she brings a loaded rifle to school to motivate her students to do work.

**Lilly Ruth Maureen Walls (Maureen)**

Rex and Rose Mary's youngest daughter, she is named after her two grandmothers Lilly and Erma Ruth.

**Miss Cook**

Jeannette's first grade teacher in Blythe, California.

**Mary Charlene Walls**

Rex and Rose Mary's second daughter, Mary Charlene dies at only 9-months old one night in her crib. Her death prompts Rex's gambling and drinking habits.

**Quixote**

The Walls' cat who has a missing ear. He is grey and white. After losing Tinkerbell, Jeannette tries to play with Quixote but the cat scratches and growls at her. This prompts Mr. Walls to throw the cat out of the car, abandoning him in Arizona.

**Lori Walls**

Rex and Rose Mary's first child, Lori is born bald and mute until her third year when she her red hair begins to grow and she begins speaking. As eldest, she often takes charge of the household when neither Rex nor Rose Mary is up to the job.

## Brian Walls

Jeannette's younger brother. When he is born Brian is seizing and his skin is blue from lack of oxygen. He seldom whines or cries and has a tough demeanor. Like other Walls children, Brian has red hair. He also has freckles on his nose. Brian is very protective of his sister Lori and likes to play in nature. He loses faith in his father at a young age.

## Rose Mary Walls

Jeannette's mother. Rose Mary enjoys art and dislikes rules. She frequently withdraws into her own world and is incredibly self-involved, sometimes to the point of placing her children in harm. She calls herself an "excitement addict" and is most pleased when life is an adventure.

## Rex Walls

Jeannette's father. Jeannette describes him as smelling like cigarettes, whisky, and hair tonic. Rex invents credentials in order to get jobs, which he never keeps for long. A dreamer, Mr. Walls creates many fantastical stories to explain realities of life to his children. For instance, when they have to move because of bill collectors, Rex instead tells his children that they are being chased by FBI agents. Rex is plagued by drunkenness and gambling addictions.

## JuJu

The black mutt Jeannette's family owned when they lived in Southern Arizona. JuJu's death leads to Jeannette's first memory of her brother Brian crying.

## Jeannette Walls

The main character and author of the memoir, Jeannette is a hard-working and intelligent child. She is the favorite child of her father, Rex and she is able to believe in him for the longest out of all the children. Jeanette becomes a journalist later in life and is married twice.

## John

Jeannette's second husband. She falls madly in love with John who also moved around a lot in his childhood and whose mother grew up in an Appalachian village not far from Welch.

# Major Themes

### Fire

Fire resurfaces frequently as a theme in *The Glass Castle*. As Jeannette suspects, it follow her around, becoming a fixture in her life. The very first, and perhaps most pivotal fire inspires Jeannette's first memory, of being burned while cooking hot dogs at the age of three. Though she suffers extreme injuries, fire becomes a fixation for Jeannette, who cannot keep herself from playing with it and watching it. The work contains a number of other fires that claim houses, sheds, and injure other characters. It can be said to represent a trend of chaos that is both natural and staged by man. The theme of fire relates closely to other themes concerning nature and pollution that also appear in the memoir.

### Bended Joshua Tree

The tree that Rose Mary spots in the desert is indicative of the effect the struggles of life have on each of the characters in the memoir. Constantly blown by wind, the Joshua tree grows sideways, not upwards and, as Rose Mary declares, becomes beautiful because of its struggle. The Walls children can be seen as individual Joshua trees, their lives shaped by the constantly blowing wind of their parents' frequent moves and questionable habits. Jeannette tries to resist this force at first when living in New York. She does not want anyone to know about her past or judge her for allowing her parents to remain homeless. However, her attempts to grow upwards despite the constantly blowing wind are averted and she eventually succumbs like the Joshua tree, and grows sideways, finally allowing her struggle to be heard.

### Mountain Goat

Rex's nickname for his favorite child. The nickname refers to Jeannette's endurance in face of trouble. Like a mountain goat, she is able to climb mountains without losing her footing. Jeannette is the only child given a nickname by her father. The endearment implies a special relationship between her and her father that the other children could not share with Rex. Additionally, the nickname foreshadows Jeannette's persistence and endurance when she realizes that her and her siblings must live apart from their parents if they are to ever lead stable, fulfilling lives.

### "Perversion of Nature"

Especially during the time they spend in the desert, the Walls place a huge emphasis on nature being corrupted by man. Even the most natural scenes are often interrupted by a structure that would not be there but for the needs of man. When Brian and Jeannette run into the lettuce field after scaring away the bullies, they are sprayed by pesticide. Not knowing (or perhaps not caring) the two continue to frolic and rejoice in the field. Again, during their play Brian and

Jeannette encounter hazardous and toxic waste in the dump. The presence of this man-made material amidst nature creates dangerous, almost fatal circumstances for the two. While Rose Mary and Rex definitely see some of these products of technological civilization as a "perversion of nature", like the irrigation in Battle Mountain, Jeannette does not always remember it that way. Indeed, often the "perversions" like the pesticide and toxic waste add a bit of magic and adventure to her memories. Only presently do the circumstances appear particularly dangerous.

## "Boundary Between Turbulence and Order"

Rex describes this concept of physics after Brian and Jeannette almost die in a fire they set while playing with toxic waste. He warns them that no rules exist in the Boundary between turbulence and order and that if they do, nobody yet understands them. That day he says they have gotten too close to the boundary. In a way, the Walls children live in perpetual proximity to this boundary. After Rex begins drinking heavily and there is no food in the house, they begin scavenging for food and clothing through various means and enter into a place where rules and order no longer exist. The Boundary reappears at the end of the novel when Jeannette remarks that the flame of the candle is bordering the boundary between turbulence and order. This suggests a relation between this boundary and the ever-present fires of the novel; both represent chaos and control throughout the work.

## Self Sufficiency

Even during their hardest times, Rex and Rose Mary Walls refuse to become charity cases. They do not even accept help from their children in their late adulthood. The value of being self sufficient descends mainly from Rose Mary Walls, whose upbringing in an incredibly disciplined home leads her to forgo the rules when she becomes a mother. Her children, she insists, must learn how to be self sufficient and strong. They should not rely on society or doctors or anything else to help them through life. Even when they fall ill or injure themselves, Rose Mary prefers to treat the wound at home rather than cater to what she considers a false need to visit the hospital. Though the Walls value self sufficiency they are not always able to maintain it, and sometimes their methods are not sufficient for survival at all.

## Nonconformity

Rex and Rose Mary Walls also insist that their children are special and that they need not conform to the societal norm. Rex is even a little saddened when his son Brian joins the Air Force, what Rex considers "the gestapo." Nonconformity also impacts the elder Walls' relation to authority. Neither of them is capable of taking orders from authority very well. Rex gets into arguments and fights with bosses and law enforcement, and Rose Mary struggles to conform to the idea of a teaching job. She prefers the carefree and self-defined life as an artist, which does not force her to conform to another person's style or schedule beside her own.

## The Glass Castle

The title of the book and a major theme within it, the Glass Castle represents Rex's hope for a magical, fantastic life in which he can provide for his family and please his children. Rex lays out plans for the Glass Castle, including detailed dimensions for each of the children's rooms, but he never actually builds the castle. For a long time Jeannette believes that he will but she gives up on the hope after the hole they dig for the foundation of the Glass Castle is filled with garbage. Though the physical structure is not erected, the symbol the Glass Castle represents remains with Jeannette in her childhood and helps her to believe that her father will do what he promises. When she discovers that this is not always true and realizes that the Glass Castle will never actually be built, she has reached adulthood.

# Glossary of Terms

**Benighted**
Ignorant.

**Blasphemy**
Disrespectful or irreverent actions towards sacred objects or figures.

**Cantankerous**
Argumentative, Characterized by a bad temper.

**Convoluted**
Complex; hard to follow; not clear.

**Ergo**
Refers to the conclusion of an earlier argument in logic.

**Felonious**
Relating to a crime. Criminal.

**Genuflect**
Bend the knee to the ground. Frequently used in reference to prayer.

**Geodes**
Rocks made from the lava of volcanoes. They have hollow insides and around the interior there are white crystals or purple amethysts. Geodes are Jeannette's favorite type of rock to collect.

**Gestate**
The process of carrying a being in the womb.

**Glowering**
Scowling, Staring with an angry look on one's face.

**Indignant**
Feeling annoyed by supposed unfair treatment.

**Mantilla**
Lace scarf worn over the head. Popular in Spain and is most often worn by women during traditional Catholic practices.

## Oompahing

Sound made by a brass instrument such as a tuba. Characterized by a steady rhythm.

## Ornate

Designed intricately with much detail; showy.

## Serape

A shawl-like cloth worn mainly in Mexico.

## Simony

Making a profit by selling sacred things. Often used in reference to the church and its members.

## The Green Lantern

A house of prostitution near the highway Battle Mountain. Rose Mary calls the place a "cathouse" in which bad things happen but Jeannette and Brian are confused since they see no cats. Intrigued, Jeannette dares Brian to go up to the porch of the Green Lantern. Brian acquiesces and speaks to one of the women who explains that the Green Lantern is a place where men come and are treated nicely by women. After that day the women in the Green Lantern continue to wave at Brian though Jeannette continues to keep her distance.

## Treadle

A pedal or lever operated by the foot as can be found on a sewing machine.

## Usury

Charging interest on loans.

## Warmonger

A negative term for an individual who wants to motivate a nation to enter into warfare.

# Short Summary

*The Glass Castle* details the story of Jeannette Walls and her family. Constantly short on cash and food, the family moves around the country frequently and tries to re-settle. Though the family is dysfunctional, the memoir communicates itself without condemning either of the Walls parents. Humor frequently imbues the work with a light-spirited tone.

For the first half of the work, the family lives in various mining towns on the West Coast of America. This part of the work is characterized by frequent moves from town to town. As Jeannette grows up in the desert she is enchanted by the limitless bounds of nature and the fantasies her father dreams up for her and her siblings. While living in the desert Jeannette begins a rock collection and explores the natural and man-made features of the environment with her brother Brian. Life in the desert ends when Rex's alcoholism worsens and the family runs out of funds. They leave the desert and relocate to Welch, West Virginia, the town where Rex grew up, to find better prospects.

Life in Welch, West Virginia is completely different than the life the Walls led in the desert on the West coast. Most notably, Welch has a winter season which brings new challenges to the Walls family. From their arrival, the Wells children are itching to leave Welch and return to the desert. But eventually circumstances become so bad that they realize they must move away from their parents in order to achieve stable lives. Lori and Jeannette set their sights on New York and begin saving money to move out of Welch once and for all.

Eventually the siblings all end up relocating from Welch to New York in an attempt to be liberated from the stifling environment in Welch. For a time everyone is settled and living independently until Rex and Rose Mary show up in Manhattan in a van. After just a short while, the couple ends up poor and homeless once again and despite their efforts, the children are unable to take on the burden of hosting their parents anymore. Consequently, Rose Mary and Rex become squatters in abandoned apartments until Rex dies after having a heart attack.

By the memoir's end, Jeannette has finally reconciled her past and present and no longer feels the need to hide behind lies or half-truths. The memoir liberates her and allows her to do what she enjoys most about writing; communicate with the world.

# Quotes and Analysis

*Until then, when I thought of writers, what first came to mind was Mom, hunched over her typewriter, clattering away on her novels and plays and philosophies of life and occasionally receiving a personalized rejection letter. But a newspaper reporter, instead of holing up in isolation, was in touch with the rest of the world. What the reporter wrote influenced what people thought about and talked about the next day; he knew what was really going on. I decided I wanted to be one of the people who knew what was really going on.*

*204*

In seventh grade Jeannette is the first person her age to work for the school newspaper, *The Maroon Wave*. She seeks it out as a place where she can belong and have an identity without worrying about people teasing her for being poor or dirty or criticizing her parents. During her work with the school newspaper Jeannette discovers what she wants to do with her life and what she later ends up doing: journalism. It is important that she not keep her work to herself or experience it alone, like her mother, but rather that it exist as a dialogue between her and the rest of the world.

*If you don't want to sink, you better figure out how to swim.*

*66*

Rex teaches Jeannette how to swim by literally forcing her to sink or swim. He repeatedly throws her into a sulfur spring in the desert, rescuing her when she sinks only to throw her back in again. Using these methods, Rex is able to train Jeannette to paddle and swim in order to avoid being thrown back into the water. This strategy is representative of Rose Mary and Rex's general approach to parenting. Refusing to coddle their children, they often present them with challenges, some life threatening, that the children are forced to handle.

*I wondered if the fire had been out to get me. I wondered if all fire was related, like dad said all humans were related, if the fire that had burned me that day while I cooked hot dogs was somehow connected to the fire I had flushed down the toilet and the fire burning at the hotel. I didn't have the answers to those questions, but what I did know was that I lived in a world that at any moment could erupt into fire. It was the sort of knowledge that kept you on your toes.*

*34*

After the hotel where they are staying burns down, a young Jeannette begins to think that fire is a recurring part of her life. She believes that her encounters with fire are all connected and impacted by each other. Most importantly, she realizes that her life is unpredictable and her status transient. Fire is sudden and damaging and capable of changing the trajectory of one's life in an instant. Jeannette's early experiences with fire foreshadow the combustive events to follow in her life.

*Mom frowned at me. 'You'd be destroying what makes it special' she said, 'It's the Joshua tree's struggle that gives it its beauty'.*

38

When Jeannette devises a plan to aright the Joshua tree which has grown sideways in the direction of the constant wind that passes over it, her mother quickly dismisses the idea. Rose Mary claims that the tree is beautiful not because it grows straight like the other trees, but rather because its struggle defines it and makes it unique. Rose Mary is typically unwilling to tamper with nature and she is particularly drawn to the unique form of the Joshua Tree. Through the figure of the tree a young Jeannette learns an important lesson about non-conformity.

*After dinner the whole family stretched out on the benches and the floor of the depot and read, with the dictionary in the middle of the room so we kids could look up words we didn't know...Occasionally, on those nights when we were all reading together, a train would thunder by, shaking the house and rattling the windows. The noise was thunderous, but after we'd been there a while, we didn't even hear it.*

56-57

This scene depicts one of the few peaceful, bonding moments shared between members of the Wells family. Not coincidentally, the family bonds around literature and reading. The importance of this scene is two-fold. Firstly, it debunks stereotypes about the homeless being uneducated or dumb and shows that even those without means can be learned. Secondly, it shows how Jeannette becomes influenced at a young age by the written word and is a possible explanation for her later interest in journalism. It is the parents' literary bent that ultimately saves the children, by giving them the education that allows them to escape their parents' life.

*We're not poor.*

121

When the Walls receive a ride from a stranger after their vehicle breaks down on the highway, Jeannette is annoyed by the tone of the woman who offers to drive them home. She is particularly put off by the woman's frequent use of the word 'poor' to describe the family. Attempting to defend the dignity of her parents and siblings, Jeannette firmly asserts that the family is not poor and the woman quickly apologizes. Following this incident, Jeannette begins to define herself apart from her and her family's situation and she refuses to accept the disdain presented to her by some members of society.

*Situations like these, I realized, were what turned people into hypocrites*

*144*

Jeannette stands up to her grandmother, Erma when she questions Jeannette's friendship with a African American classmate. When Erma gets angry, Jeannette is surprised that her parents aren't more supportive of her bravery in countering authority. Rex and Rose Mary are less concerned about Jeannette learning non-conformist practices as they are afraid that they will be kicked out of Erma's home. As a result, they chastise their daughter for angering her grandmother. After this incident, Jeannette realizes that even her parents can be forced to conform if the consequences of rebelling are severe enough.

'Oh Yeah?' I said. 'How about Hitler?What was his redeeming quality?'

'Hitler loved dogs,' Mom said without hesitation.

*144*

Rose Mary tries to teach Jeannette a lesson in compassion. She explains that even the worst of people have good qualities. Jeannette is frustrated with the prejudice of her grandmother towards Blacks but Rose Mary encourages Jeannette to instead find her grandmother's positive traits and understand the upbringing that indoctrinated her with such hateful ideas. She wants Jeannette to understand, not judge.

Later that night, Dad stopped the car out in the middle of the desert, and we slept under the stars. We had no pillows, but Dad said that was part of his plan. He was teaching us to have good posture. The Indians didn't use pillows, either, he explained, and look how straight they stood. We did have our scratchy army-surplus blankets, so we spread them out and lay there, looking up at the field of stars. I told Lori how lucky we were to be sleeping out under the sky like Indians.

'We could live like this forever,' I said.

'I think we're going to,' she said.

*18*

This passage illustrates a number of important characterizations in the memoir. Rex, is always dreaming up fantastic alternatives to reality to make life more adventurous for his children. Rex communicates serious situations as privileges and excitement. Jeannette is the only one who plays along with these fantasies of her father's. She believes the words he says, or at least, at a later age, the intent behind them. Though this is early in the memoir, already Lori shows signs of cynicism. She has already stopped believing fully in her father's fantasies and instead sees the reality of their circumstances.

Mom pointed her chopsticks at me. 'You see?' she said. 'Right there. That's exactly what I'm saying. You're way too easily embarrassed. Your father and I are who we are. Accept it.'

'And what am I supposed to tell people about my parents?'

'Just tell the truth,' Mom said. 'That's simple enough.'

5

This conversation takes place immediately before Jeannette's description of her childhood. Her mother behaves almost like a muse invoking Jeannette's story and giving her the confidence to tell it. This quote also reveals some of Jeannette's apprehensions about letting her colleagues and friends know the truth about her life growing up. Even in adulthood, she has a hard time accepting the truth of her upbringing and fears that the past will somehow damage her present happiness.

# Summary and Analysis of Part 1: A Woman on the Street

## Summary

On an evening in March Jeannette Walls is riding in a taxi headed to a party when she sees her mother digging through a trashcan. Walls has not seen her mother for months and she is struck by the reality that the woman who raised her presently appears no different to passersby than any other homeless person on the city streets. Indeed, many of those walking down the street pass the woman without acknowledging her existence. From the confines of the taxi car, Walls observes the familiar mannerisms of her mother and is reminded of the woman who played with her during childhood and read her Shakespeare stories, the woman who was now rummaging through a dumpster in the East Village.

However, Jeannette quickly curtails her reminiscence out of fear that someone will notice her. Only a few blocks away from the party, she fears that her fixation on the woman by the dumpster would arouse suspicion. To avoid being seen she lowers herself in her seat and tells the taxi driver to take her to her home on Park Avenue. She cannot risk being seen by any other attendees of the party lest they discover her 'secret', that she is the daughter of a homeless woman in New York. The driver turns around and Walls, like the strangers on the street, passes by her mother without saying anything to her.

When Walls returns to her apartment she feels ashamed for hiding from her mother. She is also stricken by guilt for having furniture, antiques, and jewelry when her parents do not even have a constant source of food or a permanent residence. But Walls tempers her guilt by recalling her previous attempts to help her parents. Walls remembers that any attempt to reach out in the past resulted in stubborn denials from her parents who did not even acknowledge that they needed help. When her offers were accepted, Jeannette's mother often asked for extravagant and unnecessary items like membership to a fitness club. Nevertheless, Walls is so ashamed of her behavior that she decides to invite her mother to lunch at a Chinese restaurant. However, communicating the invite is no easy feat. Walls must first leave a message at another woman's house (a friend of her mother's) and wait a few days for her mother to get the message and respond.

As predicted, during lunch Jeannette's mother first denies that she needs help from her daughter and then requests electrolysis treatment. Frustrated, Jeannette insists that her mother improve the quality of her life but her mother quickly refuses, accusing Jeannette of being the one in need of help since her "values are all confused". She accuses Jeannette of having "confused" values once again after discovering what happened the night Jeannette hid in the taxi. She says that instead of hiding her past and being embarrassed, Jeannette ought to instead tell the truth.

## Analysis

The memoir's beginning lays bare all of Jeannette's hitherto pent up insecurities about her troubled past. Though she has escaped the substandard circumstances that characterized her childhood, Rose Mary's appearance by the dumpster is a symbol that Jeannette cannot ever fully hide from her past life of poverty and periodic homelessness. The story and the fear of it being discovered could always be lurking behind any city corner.

The title of the section alone resurrects the lurking feeling of shame Jeannette felt before embarking on this project. Entitled, "A Woman on the Street", the section contains no direct reference to Rose Mary Walls nor does it outright acknowledge the relation between the "woman on the street" and the author of the book.

The discussion about values resurfaces throughout Jeannette's memoirs. Already, conventional understandings of "confused" and stable values are challenged when Jeannette meets with her mother. This foreshadows Jeannette's story and the actions of her parents which are not always so definitively good or bad, right or wrong. This initial discussion changes the framework for the reader, preparing her to enter a world in which the person rooting through the dumpster may have more secure values than the one living in a Park Avenue apartment.

The structure of Part I reveals Jeannette's secret while also telling the reader that she made it out. A well known journalist living in Park Avenue, the Jeannette Walls of Part I seems like she would have very little to do with the young Jeannette Walls of the following chapters, the Jeannette Walls who was sometimes forced to rummage through dumpsters for food or to eat maggot-infested meat when nothing else was available.

The structure also imitates that of more classical forms as Rose Mary functions as a muse, speaking to the writer and inspiring her work. Rose Mary's final words to Jeannette during their meal together urge her to tell the truth and to stop hiding. As if propelled by these words of her mother, Jeannette launches directly into the memoir, no longer afraid to be found out by her colleagues and friends.

# Summary and Analysis of Part 2: The Desert

## Summary

At her home in Southern Arizona, three-year old Jeannette Walls' pink dress catches fire while she is cooking hot dogs in her family's trailer. The account is described as the author's first memory. Upon hearing her child's screams, Jeannette's mother rushes in from the other room and puts out the flames with a wool blanket. She then grabs Jeannette and her younger son, Brian, and goes to the neighboring trailer to ask for a ride to the hospital. Jeannette's injuries are serious but the doctors are able to treat the burns by giving her a series of skin grafts, replacing the burned skin on her upper body with skin from her upper thigh. However, the nature of the accident prompts the doctors to ask Jeannette a series of questions about her life at home, particularly how it is that she was allowed to use the stove at such a young age. A young Jeannette answers matter-of-factly, asserting that her mother allowed her to cook often because she was 'mature for [her] age'.

Jeannette enjoys the solitude and order of the hospital, qualities which do not characterize her home life. And she is excited to finally have a room to herself, instead of having to share one with her brother and sister. In the hospital Jeannette is first introduced to chewing gum by one of the nurses. Yet, Mr. and Mrs. Walls are not so pleased and they do not hide their disdain for the hospital and its staff. Mrs. Walls is upset that the nurse gave her daughter chewing gum without asking permission and Mr. Walls is unimpressed by the " 'med-school quacks'" that run the hospital. They tell Jeannette about a time when Lori, their eldest daughter, was stung by a scorpion in the desert and instead of taking her to the hospital they took her to a Navajo witch-doctor. Mr. Walls remarks that they should have done the same with Jeannette after her injury. The Walls' dislike for hospitals is made more apparent when Brian falls off a couch and bloodies his head and Mr. and Mrs. Walls bandage it up themselves instead of taking him to a doctor. At one point Mr. Walls becomes so confrontational with the hospital staff that he is forcibly removed by hospital security. Soon afterward, escaping the hospital (and the accompanying hospital bill), Mr. Walls removes his daughter from her hospital bed without receiving clearance to do so.

After returning from the hospital, Jeannette becomes enthralled by fire. Her parents support this, insistent that she not be defeated or afraid of that which led to her injury. Not only does Jeannette resume cooking hot dogs on the stove (to the delight of her mother) but she also starts to steal her father's matches. One day while playing with matches she accidentally burns her favorite toy, a Tinkerbell figurine, distorting the doll's face irreparably. Though Tinkerbell remains her favorite toy, Jeannette expresses hope that she could have given Tinkerbell skin graft surgery the way the doctors did for her.

The family has to move suddenly one night and in the rush Jeannette forgets to pack Tinkerbell. She hopes that Tinkerbell's new owner will like her despite her melted face. The "skedaddle", as Jeannette describes the move, is common for the Walls family, and is often characterized by a stealthy escape late in the night. Mr. Walls explains the need for such hasty relocation to his children by telling them that someone is after them, FBI agents or big business executives. Mrs. Walls corrects him, explaining to her children that they were in fact being pursued by bill collectors, not federal agents.

During these years the Walls family frequently relocates. They live temporarily in Arizona, Nevada, and California where Mr. Walls takes manual labor jobs until he is fired or the bill collectors come after them. When this happens the family moves again. On occasion the Walls stay with Grandma Smith, Rose Mary's mother. However, these visits are frequently cut short when Rex and Grandma Smith get into an argument about her being uppity and him being unable to take care of his family. After such arguments, the family packs up once again in search of yet another mining town.

Both Rose Mary and Jeannette enjoy life in the desert. They find pleasure in the sandstorms, the rainstorms, and the wildlife. Rose Mary, having grown up in the desert, is particularly skilled at helping her family to survive. The children are home schooled by their parents and they are careful not to make any real attachments to the other children because they always know they will move again.

One day Rex announces plans to finally settle the family in one place for awhile. According to him, the family can stop moving from place to place as soon as he finds gold. In pursuit of gold, Rex begins working on an invention called 'The Prospector', a design intended to sift through sand detecting and separating gold nuggets from rocks and dirt by measuring the weight of each gathered piece.

Rex tells his children that once the Prospector is finished he will begin building the 'Glass Castle', a house with glass walls and ceilings, even a glass staircase, where the family can live and each of the children can have their own rooms.

Rex also promises to replace his wife's wedding ring once he finds enough gold. He had pawned the ring off for cash after squandering the family's funds on alcohol and gambling, habits Rex adopted after finding his daughter Mary Charlene dead in her crib one night. That incident forever changed Rex, plaguing him with dark moods and periodic drinking, but it did not affect Mrs. Wells nearly as badly. She saw Mary Charlene's death as a sign of God's protection, he only took her away because she was imperfect, but he blessed her with three other perfect children: Lori, Brian, and Jeannette.

Rex moves his family to Las Vegas in the hopes that he will make some money at the casinos. While he and his wife are gambling the children discuss their feelings about moving around so frequently. Jeannette says that she likes moving around and asks what would happen if they stayed in one place instead. Lori guesses that if they did that they would "get caught." While driving away from the casino, Jeannette falls out of the side door of the car and tumbles down a desert hill, bloodying her nose and getting pebbles and debris stuck in her skin. She waits for a long time by the place where she fell, fearing that her parents might abandon her. When her family finally returns, Jeannette refuses a hug from her father, blaming him for trying to leave her behind forever. However, her mood is lightened when Rex, trying to treat Jeannette's various injuries calls her nose a "snot locker", which she finds hilarious.

The family has to leave Las Vegas after the casino owners discover Rex has been cheating at the blackjack table. They settle for a time in San Francisco until the hotel they are living in catches fire. Jeannette begins to think that fire is a recurring part of her life. She wonders whether the hotel fire is related to the fires she set while playing with matches or the fire that burned her when she was cooking hot dogs. After San Francisco the Walls live in a place called Midland which they discover after Rose Mary demands that they stop in the area so she can paint a Joshua tree that has grown sideways, in the direction of the wind that constantly blew against it. In Midland the family dog, Juju, dies after being bitten by a rattlesnake, which makes Brian cry for the first time Jeannette can remember. Rex is employed as a gypsum miner and Rose Mary delves into her artwork. She discovers that she is pregnant and hopes for a boy so Brian will have a playmate.

That Christmas, the family has no money because Rex is fired from his mining job after arguing with the foreman. Instead of getting the children toys which he cannot afford, Rex takes them out to the desert and tells each of them to pick out a star. Lori chooses Betelgeuse, Brian, Rigel, and Jeannette chooses a planet, Venus. The children are pleased to have gotten stars instead of toys and they feel proud not to have been deceived by the myth of Santa Claus like the other kids.

Rex and Rose Mary get into a heated argument while the family is moving from Midland to Blythe. Rex, who had drank some Tequila earlier in the day, is frustrated by Rose Mary's insistence that she carried Lori in her womb for 14 months. He tells her that she simply lost count of the months. Offended by Rex's hostility, Rose Mary jumps out of the moving vehicle. Rex chases her in the car, cursing at her as he drives, and the children are afraid he is going to run her over. Eventually Rex corners Rose Mary by some rocks and tosses her back into the car. Though Rose Mary sobs for the remainder of the car ride, the next day the couple has made up.

In Blythe the family lives in the 'LBJ Apartments', which Jeannette believes stands for the 'Lori, Brian, Jeannette Apartments', with a large population of Spanish speaking migrant workers. Jeannette attends first grade and is such a good student that the other students begin calling her teacher's pet. Four girls beat her up after school, giving her a busted lip and prompting Brian to begin watching out for his sister after school. Brian attempts to scare the girls away but both he and Jeannette are beaten up by them. Nevertheless, the pair is proud to have stood up to the bullies. In Blythe, Rose Mary gives birth to another girl who she names Lilly Ruth Maureen, after her mother Lilly and Rex's mother, Erma Ruth.

A police car tries to pull over the family because the car's brake lights aren't working. Afraid that the police will discover that they have neither registration nor insurance and that the license plate was stolen from another vehicle, Rex outruns the police car and decides that the family must leave Blythe. They head for Battle Mountain, a place in Nevada where Rex claims there is gold to be found. The family must rent a U-Haul to travel the 14 hours to Battle Mountain and the children, including newborn Maureen, are forced to sit in the cold and dark storage area of the truck. During the ride the back doors swing open and the children must cling to the tied down furniture in order to stay in the U-Haul. A passing car signals to Rex that the door is open and when he pulls the truck over he is both angered at his children and scared by the thought of what could have happened to them.

When they arrive in Battle Mountain the family settles into a building that once served as a railroad depot. They use spools from the rail yard as tables and chairs and the children sleep in boxes. When they overhear their parents talking about buying beds for them they protest, claiming that sleeping in boxes makes sleep more adventurous. Rex begins works in a mine as an engineer and stops going out to drink after work. Instead, he and his family read works by Dickens, Faulkner, Pearl Buck and others, with a dictionary in the center of the room for looking up words the kids didn't recognize. Jeannette begins second-grade at the Mary S. Black Elementary School and continues to perform well ahead of the rest of her classmates.

Jeannette begins a rock collection and she and Brian also begin playing in the dump. One day they try to make explosions out of some toxic wastes they find in the dump and they accidentally set a wooden shed aflame. Jeannette runs out but Brian insists that they put out the fire to avoid getting into trouble. Coincidentally, Rex is walking along the path beside the shed when Jeannette runs out looking for help. Rex pulls Brian out of the burning shed and soberly tells the children that they made a bad decision, getting too close to the boundary between turbulence and order, "a place where no rules apply".

While at her friend Carla's house Jeannette discovers that Carla does not have pests or animals in her home, but the Walls' house is full of stray cats and dogs, lizards, snakes, and other animals. She asks Carla's mother how they keep their house animal free and she says that she uses a No-Pest Strip to keep critters out. When Jeannette tells her mother this, Rose Mary refuses to buy one, declaring that anything that kills animals probably isn't healthy for them either. That winter, Rex purchases a Ford Fairlane and takes the kids to swim in the Hot Pot, a sulfur spring composed of warm, smelly water and bordered by quicksand and mineral deposits. Rex forces Jeannette to learn how to swim in the Hot Pot by throwing her in and letting her sink before rescuing her and throwing her back in again. Though she learns how to swim, Jeannette is initially angered at her father for his tactics and at the rest of her family for allowing him to use them. Her anger subsides when her father tells her that she learned an important lesson in addition to learning how to swim: "you can't cling to the side your whole life".

After six-months living in Battle Mountain, Rex loses his job at the mine. He devotes his free time to perfecting the prospector and looking for gold. As a result, the family has very little to eat and the children are forced to scavenge food from neighbors. Jeannette sneaks food from her classmates' lunch boxes at recess. Brian gets caught stealing a jar of pickles from a neighbor and is forced to eat the entire jar until he is sick. One evening, Rose Mary gets angry at Jeannette for eating the last stick of butter and when Jeannette defends her actions, saying that she was hungry, Rose Mary begins to cry and confesses that she doesn't like living in poverty either. That night, Rex and Rose Mary get into a rowdy fight which draws the entire neighborhood out of their homes. Rex tells Rose Mary to ask her mother to invest money in the Prospector and demands that she get a job if she doesn't like their lifestyle. The fight ends dramatically with Rose Mary hanging out of the upstairs window, Rex holding her from inside of the house. Rose Mary claims that Rex attempted to kill her but Rex swears he did no such thing. The next day Rose Mary applies for a teaching position at the Battle Mountain Intermediate School and is hired immediately.

Rose Mary begins teaching Lori's class but she is criticized by the principal for allowing her class to descend into disorder and for not disciplining her students. Rose Mary does not like teaching because it was what her mother told her she would have to do if being an artist did not work out. Teaching, then, was a representation of Rose Mary's failure as an artist, which made her unenthusiastic and unmotivated to do her job. Though they knew she did not enjoy it, the Walls children did their best to prevent their mother from getting fired. They woke her up in time for school, helped her to grade papers, and whenever the principal stopped by the classroom Rose Mary showed that she could discipline students by always yelling at Lori so she could spare the other children.

Though Rose Mary is the only one employed, Rex insists on maintaining control over the family's finances. Despite Rose Mary's efforts to save, every month he is able to get possession of her earnings. Rex is quick to spend the money on liquor or big meals at the Owl Club and Brian and Lori are frustrated by his wastefulness. Jeannette tries to defend her father to her siblings because she knows Rex considers her his favorite but Lori and Brian insist that their father needs to start contributing to the household instead of draining the money away. Brian stops waving to the women in the Green Lantern after his father takes him out one night with Ginger, a woman from the Green Lantern. It is Brian's birthday and Rex buys him a Sad Sack comic book and takes him out to dinner with the woman, Ginger. When they go to the hotel Rex and the woman disappear for awhile while Brian sits outside reading his comic book over and over again. When the woman emerges from the bedroom, she appears interested in the comic book and Rex makes Brian give the comic to her. He forever resents Ginger and the woman of the Green Lantern. Jeannette suspects that Brian has discovered out what it is about the women in the Green Lantern that is so "bad," though she is still unsure what it is.

Soon after Jeannette turns eight, Billy Deel and his father move to Battle Mountain. Billy is eleven and had spent some time in a juvenile facility for shoplifting and vandalizing property. He is attracted to Jeannette and begins calling her his girlfriend. Jeannette agrees to be his friend but refuses to be his girlfriend. Billy gives Jeannette a turquoise ring which she accepts although she still refuses to be his girlfriend. Nevertheless, Billy brags to the other children that he and Jeannette are going to get married. One day, while Jeannette is playing hide and seek with the other children, Billy squeezes himself into her hiding spot, a small shed, and forces her to kiss him. He removes his pants and reaches for her shorts but luckily the other children hear the struggle and interrupt. Later, Jeannette returns the ring and tells Billy that she wants nothing to do with him. In retaliation, Billy shows up at the Walls' house one night and shoots into the room with a BB gun. Because neither of their parents are home, Lori is in charge. She decides to retrieve her father's gun and she shoots at Billy once to get him to leave them alone. Jeannette seizes the gun and shoots at Billy again until he runs away. When their parents return they are accompanied by a police officer who tells the family that they must report to court the following morning to see the magistrate. That night the Walls "skedaddle" once again and leave for Phoenix. Each of the children is only allowed to bring one thing and Jeannette is upset to leave Battle Mountain, which had become like a home for her.

Jeannette asks if they will stay with Grandma Smith again, who lives in Phoenix. Rose Mary curtly answers that they will not because Grandma died of Leukemia. Jeannette is shocked to hear the news and angered that her mother hadn't mentioned it beforehand. She begins to punch her mother's shoulder until her father pulls her hand away. Rose Mary says that they will live in one of the houses that Grandma Smith bequeathed to her in her death, an adobe house near Phoenix's business district. There, Rose Mary will be able to begin an art studio and purchase supplies with her inheritance money.

The house that Rose Mary inherits from her mother on North Third Street is very large. It consists of fourteen rooms, a piano, a set of china, and a front and back yard. Instead of sending her children to the neighborhood Catholic school, Rose Mary arranges for them to attend the out of district public school, Emerson. There, all of the Walls children are placed into gifted reading groups. The school nurse notifies the Walls that Lori needs glasses. Begrudgingly Rose Mary allows her daughter to wear the glasses, which are provided by the school, although she considers them a "crutch". With the glasses Lori is able to see the world anew. She is moved to tears at the sight of all the details in the world that had hitherto appeared as blurs to her. After receiving her new sight, Lori decides that she will become an artist like her mother. In Phoenix Rex gets a job as an electrician and joins the union. The influx of money brings new amenities to the Walls home including bicycles for the children, telephones, a washing machine, and a record player. When roaches and termites begin to crop up in the home, Rose Mary and Rex refuse to use more conventional means of exterminating the creatures. Instead the family attacks the roaches using rolled up newspapers and Rex fills the termite created holes with empty beer cans.

Rex is fired three times before he is kicked out of the electrician's union. The inheritance money has run out and, once again, food is in short supply for the Walls family. Brian and Jeannette discover a warehouse dumpster full of chocolates which they eat whenever there is no food in the house. Rose Mary recruits the children for a shoplifting scheme to get Maureen new clothes for preschool and Rex discovers a sly way to withdraw twice as much money from the bank by making withdrawals from the teller and drive-thru window simultaneously. After losing his job Rex begins to drink heavily and he frequently returns home violent and angry, smashing dishes and trashing the house. Rose Mary hides from him during these episodes while the children try to calm him down. She also refuses to allow Jeannette to clean up the messes, claiming that Rex needs to see the consequences of his actions. That Christmas, Rose Mary is determined to have a traditional Catholic Christmas and takes the family to mass. Rex, who has been drinking since breakfast, has an outburst at Midnight Mass and the entire family is escorted out of the church. When they return home, Rex lights the thrift store Christmas tree on fire, destroying the tree and the ornaments as well as the family's hopes for a merry Christmas.

That spring, when Jeannette turns ten, Rex asks her what she wants for her birthday. Surprised, because birthdays are usually not celebrated and forgotten in their family, Jeannette tells her father that she wants him to stop drinking. For days Rex, lies in bed strapped to the bed posts in agony in withdrawal from alcohol. That summer, as he regains his strength, he proposes that the family take a trip to the Grand Canyon. However, on their way the car breaks down after Rex exhausts the engine trying to see how fast the car can go. The family is forced to walk home until a woman picks them up and takes them back to Phoenix. On the night of their return, Rex does not come home.

Rex does not return for another three days and when he does he is drunk and angry, shouting and cursing. He gets into a violent fight with Rose Mary . Though both of them draw knives, after Rex asks if Rose Mary loves him and she answers affirmatively, they collapse into each other's arms laughing and hugging. Rose Mary decides that the family should move to West Virginia where Rex's parents might be able to help curb his drinking habit and help the family financially. She sells some of her inherited land in Texas and buys an Oldsmobile for $200 to replace the car that broke down during their trip to the Grand Canyon. Though he is not excited about the move, Rex begrudgingly gets into the car and demands that he be permitted to drive.

**Analysis**

This section begins with the most vivid of Jeannette's early memories: the day she is set on fire at age three. The incident illustrates a few main themes of the novel. Firstly, the presence of fire is introduced in this scene. Initially, it is something that has the potential to nourish (it allows Jeannette to cook her hot dogs) but instead causes great damage to the young Jeannette's body. Secondly, the nature of the Walls' parenting becomes clear. This is a home in which three year olds are permitted to cook on the stove, in which injured youth are broken out of the hospital before the doctor clears her dismissal.

This initial clash of the Walls family with the order and cleanliness of the hospital is a telling contrast. While there, the Walls determine that they should have taken Jeannette to an Indian witch doctor instead, anywhere but the sterile and orderly hospital. Positioning the hospital as a symbol of cultural order and privilege, Jeannette shows how her parents taught their children to avoid conformity and to disdain the unnecessary frills in life. Further, the hospital illustrates the Walls' apprehensions about their children realizing that they have few means in life compared to others in society. Mr. and Mrs. Walls do not want Jeannette to receive gum from the hospital staff not because it is unhealthy for her but rather because she will know what she is missing when there is no gum regularly available to her outside the hospital.

This entrée into Jeannette's early childhood also introduces another common theme of the work: movement and mobility. The family frequently moves around to avoid paying bills or having property repossessed. Young Jeannettte learns to think of the moves as adventures when she is told by her father that they are being chased by the FBI. Though her experiences as a young child are not ideal, in a sense her conception of what was going on at the time is idealized. This contrasts with the viewpoints of Brad and Lori, Jeannette's two siblings, who seem frustrated and unenthused about the 'adventure' of moving frequently.

Character development of Jeannette's parents, Rex and Rose Mary, introduces some other major themes of the work. Rex, who always promises his family things but seldom delivers on them, is both an antagonist and a protagonist. He is a sympathetic character despite his flaws because of his charm and youthfulness. Rose Mary however is less sympathetic because she seems so self-centered. Determined to be an artist, Rose Mary declines other paying jobs even when her family needs the money for survival. Rose Mary's character also introduces larger concerns about occupations. She does not want to be a teacher or have a "real" job but rather delights in the creativity and spontaneity of being an artist.

By the section's end some of Jeannette's naiveté has faded. Having grown up in many different places, Jeannette is able to distinguish between the 'good' times and the 'bad'. She knows all families do not function as hers does. Jeannette also begins to see the harm in her father's drinking habits. When Jeannette celebrates a birthday at the end of the section, she asks her father to stop drinking. Rex tries to wean himself off the alcohol but is ultimately unsuccessful. This failure prompts the family's move back to Rex's hometown in Welch, West Virginia.

# Summary and Analysis of Part 3: Welch

## Summary

After a month of driving, the family finally makes it to Welch, West Virginia. After meeting Erma, her father's mother who refuses to be called 'Grandma,' Grandpa Walls, and Uncle Stanley, Jeannette is shocked to find no resemblance between them and her father. Welch is a picture of destitution and unemployment, though in earlier days it thrived as a coal mining town. Rex takes his family on a tour of the town and explains that the very first food stamps were handed out in Welch after hard times came to its people in the 1950's. Rose Mary sees the destitution of the town as an opportunity to establish herself as an artist since there would be no competition nearby.

Brian and Jeannette are placed in special classes for children with learning disabilities at Welch Elementary School because the principal is unable to understand their accents and they are unable to understand his. The students and teachers at Welch blame Jeannette for thinking that she is better than them. At recess, Jeannette is jumped by a crowd of girls, led by a bully named Dinitia Hewitt, but she does not tell her parents about it.

One day, Jeannette helps a young African American boy escape a dog attack. She carries him home and sees Dinitia watching her from across the street. After that, Dinitia begins to befriend Jeannette. Erma and Stanley, having prejudice towards black people, question Jeannette's choice of friends and warn her that others will consider her a "nigger lover." Jeannette and her siblings are forced to stay with their grandparents alone when Rex and Rose Mary decide to return to Phoenix to retrieve some of their things and to check on the house. While they are gone Erma tries to force herself onto Brian, claiming that his pants need mending. A fight ensues when Lori tries to get Erma to stop. When Rex returns and hears about the incident he is angry at the children and doesn't appear to care about what happened to Brian. His reaction causes Jeannette to wonder whether he was abused similarly as a child. After this, the family is kicked out of Erma and Ted's house and they must move into a dilapidated apartment at 93 Little Hobart Street which, in addition to needing numerous structural repairs, has no indoor plumbing.

Jeannette tries to fix up the home but her family is not invested in the efforts. They all seem to think that the house is damaged beyond repair. Brian and Jeannette also resume work on the Glass Castle, with the encouragement of their father. But the hole they dig for the foundation of the Glass Castle instead becomes a place for the Walls' to dump their trash, since they are unable to pay for garbage to be picked up from their home. Jeannette befriends a girl named Kathy Pastor whose mother, Ginnie Sue, works as a prostitute. When she visits, Jeannette intends to ask Ginnie Sue about her life as prostitute but she forgets and instead tells them about her life in California.

Jeannette and Brian are teased by another kid in the neighborhood, Ernie Goad. Ernie calls their family garbage and assaults Brian and Jeannette with rocks. The siblings retaliate and chase Ernie and his gang away for good by dumping a pile of rocks on them from a building roof. Rex continues to drink heavily. One night he returns with a gash on his forearm which Jeannette tries to sew up. He begins disappearing from the house for days without returning and Jeannette finds it hard to continue having faith in him.

That winter is particularly challenging because the family cannot afford to heat the house. In an attempt to start a fire with kerosene, Lori accidentally gets burned. Brian and Jeannette treat her wounds with snow but Lori develops painful blisters down her thighs. Erma Wells dies that winter. Rose Mary believes that her alcoholism was responsible for her death and consequently defines her death as suicide. Rex is upset by his family's lack of remorse for his mother's death and he disappears for days. Jeannette is sent to fetch him from one of the local pubs. Shortly after Erma's death, Uncle Stanley burns the house down after he falls asleep smoking a cigarette. He and Ted survive and are forced to relocate to a two-room apartment. On occasion, the Walls visit their apartment to use the running water. Jeannette stops making this visit however after Uncle Stanley touches her inappropriately while holding his privates. Rose Mary tells Jeannette to calm down and says sexual assault is a "crime of perception."

Jeannette and Brian discover a two-carat diamond ring in the yard outside the house. They show their mother and urge her to sell it so they can use the money for food, housing payments, and other essentials, but Rose Mary insists on keeping the ring to replace her wedding ring and to boost her self-esteem. Jeannette, who has been studying the livelihoods of other families in their neighborhood, tells Rose Mary that she needs to leave Rex so that the family can qualify for welfare. Rose Mary refuses and chastises Jeannette for losing hope in her father. Jeannette says that if she will not leave Rex then she should at least get another teaching job.

Rose Mary does not get a job right away. She only acquiesces after a child-welfare officer visits the house to see if dependent children are being neglected. Jeannette is the only one home when he arrives and she dodges his questions and tells him to return when her parents are home. She is frustrated and afraid by the visit and fears that the child-welfare officer will split up her siblings.

Although Rose Mary begins teaching regularly at Davy Elementary School just outside of Welch, the family continues to have money troubles. The money runs out every month and the children are once again forced to root through the garbage for food or subsist on nothing at all. Jeannette begins seventh grade at Welch High School that fall. She spends some time with Dinitia but not too much, because of persisting negative attitudes about racial mixing. Jeannette notices that Dinitia has changed. Later, Dinitia finds out she is pregnant and stops going to school. Jeannette discovers that Dinitia was sent to jail for stabbing her mother's boyfriend, who is likely the father of Dinitia's child and the reason for her change in demeanor.

That school year Jeannette begins working for the school newspaper, *The Maroon Wave*, where she first discovers her passion for journalism. Her faculty adviser, Miss Jeannette Bivens, was Rex's old English teacher who convinced him to stay in school and get his diploma when he was a high school student. At the newspaper Jeannette also has access to news stories from around the country and she gains a better understanding of the world.

Feeling badly about Maureen's poor upbringing, Jeannette convinces Brian and Lori to save up money to buy Maureen a gift for her seventh birthday. Maureen has grown up to a be a beautiful, blond-haired, blue-eyed girl and she spends a lot of time at friends' houses. Many of her friends have Pentecostal parents who look down on the Walls' parenting habits and Maureen adopts their beliefs, calling herself "born-again" on multiple occasions. That summer, Rose Mary goes away to renew her teaching certification and Lori is admitted to a government-run summer program for enriched children. Jeannette is left in charge of the house and she is determined to stick to a budget and feed Maureen and Brian. However, Jeannette is unable to resist her father's pleas for money and she loans him $30 dollars within a week. To earn back the money, Rex takes Jeannette out to a roadside bar where he swindles a man named Robbie in pool using Jeannette as a distraction. Afterward, Jeannette feels used by her father but when she expresses this Rex says that she was in no real harm, it was just like when he threw her into the Hot Pot; she thought she would sink but he knew she could swim.

When Lori and Rose Mary return from their summer locations both appear changed. Lori is determined to get away from Welch and her family after discovering what it is like to be treated "normal" by the kids at camp. Rose Mary has decided that she won't be teaching again but will resume her life as an artist. When Jeannette talks back to her mother, telling her that she cannot quit her teaching job because they need the money, Rose Mary asks Rex to discipline her. Jeannette tells him that he too has been shirking his parental duties and Rex gives her a whipping with his belt. After this, Jeannette resolves never to receive a whipping again and she begins to save money for her escape out of Welch.

After two filmmakers arrive in Welch as part of a government cultural enrichment program, Lori is inspired to move to New York. The filmmakers, Ken Fink and Bob Gross, insist that she will have better chances of becoming a successful artist if she moves to Manhattan. When Lori shares this plan with Jeannette, Jeannette lets her know about the escape fund and both of the girls begin contributing to it. They keep their money in a piggy bank which they name Oz. That winter, Rex arrives at home with a gold Cadillac Coupe DeVille, which he names Elvis. He won the car in a game of poker. Although Jeannette thinks they should sell the car to pay for essentials, she enjoys the feeling of riding in it and is reminded of how easy it is to move once you set your mind on doing so.

Lori begins work on her art school portfolios but she is unsuccessful. She spills coffee on he first set of work and Rex, drunk, deforms a clay bust Lori had made of

William Shakespeare. Lori becomes even more defeated when Jeannette discovers that Rex has stolen all of the escape money from Oz. After this Lori stops talking to Rex. They begin saving again but they are not able to earn nearly as much money and Lori loses morale. That summer, a family Jeannette babysits for offers her a job in Iowa, where they plan to move. Jeannette asks if Lori can take the babysitting job instead and receive a bus ticket to New York after the summer ends. The family agrees and Lori sets off for Iowa, without saying goodbye to her father.

Jeannette becomes increasingly involved in the school newspaper and is promoted to editor-in-chief by her junior year of high school. When Chuck Yeager visits Welch High School she is even permitted to conduct a one-on-one interview with him. Students stop making fun of Jeannette and begin to treat her like the cheerleaders and varsity athletes. Jeannette resolves to leave Welch after classes end to join Lori in New York City. Her father tries to entice her to stay, promising to resume work on the Glass Castle but Jeannette tells him not to bother building it for her sake; she is leaving Welch even if she has to walk to New York City. Rex walks his daughter to the bus station to see her off and he gives her his favorite jackknife for protection. From the bus, Jeannette turns around to wave goodbye to her father and wonders if she will indeed make it in the big city.

## Analysis

Racial difference becomes more pronounced when the Walls move to Welch. There, the expectation is that the races will remain separate. Though segregation is no longer legal, public facilities, like the swimming pool, maintain defacto separation. The African Americans arrive during the morning when there is no entrance fee while white people swim during the afternoon when the fee is charged. Jeannette develops a friendship with Dinitia, a black girl, which causes trouble with her Grandmother Erma and her Uncle Stanley. Jeannette defends her position that the races are not different from each other which greatly upsets her grandmother.

The move from the west to the east coast is accompanied by more than a change in racial dynamics. The Walls have to adjust to a number of things characteristic of their new environment, including the harsh winter months. The loss of the nature and warmth of the west coast, impacts the general happiness of the Walls family. Rex is defeated by having to return to the place he spent his entire childhood trying to escape, and the Walls children are ready to leave almost as soon as they arrive. Welch symbolizes the end of adventure for the Walls family, and the place from which they must all eventually escape.

93 Little Hobart Street is most symbolic of the depression that accompanies the family's move to Welch. From the outset, the house is shoddy and in desperate need of repair. However, Jeannette is the only one who tries to fix it; all other members have given up fixing or improving the house. Everyone appears hopeless that their conditions will improve and powerless to change them.

Finally, Jeannette begins to recognize that her father continually the family down. Once the only child who believed in him, she loses hope in Rex as his drunkenness worsens. When Jeannette asks Rose Mary to leave Rex so that the family can qualify for welfare, Rose Mary is shocked and she admonishes Jeannette for losing hope in her father.

The dream of the Glass Castle is also destroyed during this time. Brian and Lori begin digging a foundation for the home Rex had designed for his family, but the foundation instead becomes a ditch for garbage that the family cannot afford to have picked up. The idea and dream of the Glass Castle as a physical structure is also destroyed when this happens. Jeannette realizes that it will never be built. Yet, the Glass Castle as a symbol and an abstract hope lives on.

# Summary and Analysis of Part 4: New York City and Part 5:Thanksgiving

**Summary**

When she arrives in New York, Jeannette is greeted by Lori's friend, Evan, who picks her up from the train station and takes her to see Lori who is working a shift as a bartender at Zum Zum, a German restaurant. Jeannette goes exploring while Lori finishes her shift and decides that New Yorkers only "pretended to be unfriendly." The sisters live in Evangeline, a woman's hostel in Greenwich Village, and Jeannette gets a job working in a fast food restaurant. That summer, they move into an apartment in the South Bronx with a large Puerto Rican population. Jeannette enrolls in a public school where the students do internships instead of attending class and she begins interning at *The Phoenix*, a newspaper owned, edited, and published by a man named Mike Armstrong. She quits her job at the fast food restaurant when Mr. Armstrong offers her a full-time job working at *The Phoenix*. News comes from Brian that conditions are deteriorating in Welch, and Lori and Jeannette decide to move him up to New York as well. Soon after, Lori also petitions for Maureen to join them so that she can be better cared for. Jeannette applies and is accepted to Barnard College and the siblings begin to live a stable life as a family. Remembering their past in Welch brings them all to fits of hysteric laughter.

Three years after Jeannette left Welch, Rex and Rose Mary Walls arrive in New York in a white van, declaring they have moved permanently to New York to be a family again. The couple is kicked out of two apartments before they begin living in Lori's home. However, Lori is fed up by her father's drunken fits and her mother's aloofness and she is forced to kick them out of the apartment. Rex and Rose Mary live in the van for a time until it is towed. They become homeless. Jeanette protests her parents' new lifestyle but Rose Mary insists that "being homeless is an adventure" and refuses to do anything to change the situation.

The awareness that her parents are homeless wears on Jeannette's conscience but she is unable to appease her guilt without exposing her past to classmates and professors. Rex is hospitalized with tuberculosis and is able to stay sober for six months. This ends when he is released to work as a maintenance man in a resort upstate. Rex returns to New York City at Rose Mary's request and spends that Christmas with his family. When Jeannette tells her father she may have to drop out of Barnard because she is $1,000 dollars short of tuition money, Rex produces $950 of earnings from poker games and tells her to use it towards school. Jeannette says that they need the money more than she does but her parents insist that she take it.

After graduating from Barnard, Jeannette moves in with Eric, a man she had been dating for a long time, in an apartment on Park Avenue. She also begins working full time at the magazine she worked for during her years at Barnard. Jeannette is still unable to tell the truth about her past, afraid that it will cost her the job at the magazine. She tries to avoid conversation about her parents and when that fails she lies about them. After 4 years living together, Jeannette and Eric are married.

Uncle Jim dies and Rose Mary comes to Lori to see if she can help her purchase his plot of land back. When Rose Mary reveals that the land is worth $1 million Jeannette is shocked and wonders whether Rose Mary could have prevented their years of hunger and suffering had she simply sold the land she inherited in Texas.

Lori becomes a freelance artist and Brian joins the police force. After Maureen graduates from high school she goes to city college but she drops out and begins living with their parents in a squat and working temporarily as a bartender or a waitress. As always, Maureen depends on others to take care of her. Jeannette becomes concerned about Maureen's health when she begins exhibiting eccentric behavior. Her fears are confirmed when Maureen stabs her own mother after Rose Mary tells Maureen to move out of the house. Maureen is arrested and sentenced to time in a hospital in upstate New York. When she gets out Maureen catches a bus to California without saying goodbye to her family. Jeannette feels guilty for not protecting Maureen the way she had promised.

The family doesn't meet up as much after Maureen leaves. That moment changes things for each of them. Brian relocates to Long Island, with his wife and daughter. One day Rex calls Jeannette and asks her to come visit and to bring a gallon of vodka. Reluctantly, she arrives at their apartment on the Lower East Side where Rex announces that he is dying. Jeannette is unable to imagine life without her father but only two weeks after that visit he has a heart attack and dies, spending his last days hooked up to machines. After Rex dies Jeannette begins to feel restless and unsettled. She develops a need to always be moving, headed towards someplace instead of being there. A year later she divorces Eric, deciding that neither he nor Park Avenue were the right fit for her. She moves to an apartment on the West Side and looks forward to seeing Venus when the sky is clear enough.

*Part Five: Thanksgiving*

Five years after Rex's death the family reunites for a Thanksgiving celebration. Jeannette, and her new husband John, host them at their country home. Brian, who has also separated from his first marriage, greets them at the house with his daughter Veronica. Rose Mary brings the news that she and the squatters are finally being permitted to purchase their apartments for only $1 apiece and announces that she must return for a board meeting regarding the matter. The family drinks a toast to Rex Walls in remembrance of the man with whom "life was never boring."

**Analysis**

Mobility is repeated once again in this section. However, instead of Rex determining when and where the family will move, Jeannette and Lori take control. They become the heads of the household and rescue their own siblings from undesirable conditions in Welch. The children must "escape" from under their parents and the stifling community of Welch. The sacrifices Jeannette and Lori make--staying up until early morning to complete posters, working long hours--remind the reader of the sacrifices Rex and Rose Mary seldom made for their family.

Characterizations of Maureen as the child who needed more protection than any of the other Walls children resurfaces dramatically after the family moves to New York. In part, Maureen's characterization is set apart from that of the other Walls children because she did not remember life outside of Welch. She is always asking about California and life in the desert because she cannot remember it herself. All Maureen has to recollect is the absolute lack of adventure and excitement that existed for the family in Welch. This sense of place sets her far apart from Lori, Jeannette, and Brian. When Maureen stabs her mother, Jeannette is upset primarily with herself and her family for allowing the one who needed the most care to fall by the wayside.

Rex's gift of $950 for Jeannette's tuition is symbolic of the ways in which he was a good father. So much of the last section focuses on the intensification of Rex's drinking and gambling habits and the ways in which he brings pain to his family. However, the memoir does not characterize Rex as an exclusively negative figure. Indeed, in the final chapter he partially redeems his previous actions by offering the earnings from poker game to his daughter so that she may continue school. This incident not only pushes against conceptions of Rex as a bad person but it also challenges general stereotypes of the very poor as people who do not value education or have no skills.

Ironically, money seems to mean little to Rex and Rose Mary Walls as a means to buy necessities or to make a practical, settled life possible. Indeed, Rex's earnings at poker illustrate that he could be living in an apartment with running water were he focused on using the money towards housing. Furthermore, Rose Mary's tract of land, which Jeannette suspects might be worth one million dollars, could have dramatically altered the trajectory of life for her and her family, yet she never even considered selling it.

In the final scene of the memoir, Jeannette intentionally resurrects the memory of her father. Instead of remembering the hardships he caused the family with his alcohol and gambling addictions they instead recognize the very thing that made Rex Walls unique; his propensity for finding excitement. This scene is indicative of a larger theme in the memoir of not judging Rose Mary or Rex or criticizing them harshly. Instead, Jeannette offers her story to the reader without condemning her parents or complaining about her upbringing. Perhaps, in writing the "truth" instead of hiding from it, Jeannette is set free by it--free from shame, from the need to lie about her past, and free from any feelings of contempt that may have existed for her parents.

Summary and Analysis of Part 4: New York City and Part 5:Thanksgiving

# Suggested Essay Questions

1. Discuss the role of fire in the novel.

   After Jeannette is burned the first time fire continues to appear in the work. It burns down a number of houses and harms some of the characters. Jeannette believes that the fires might all be connected. Jeannette describes fire as a sort of character itself.

2. How does Jeannette characterize her parents? What is her tone towards them and their actions?

   Jeannette describes her parents' faults and shortcomings but she does not condemn them for their actions. Indeed, by the novel's end she appears to have come to an understanding about their way of living. The goal of the work is not to insult or vilify her parents but, in a way, to honor them.

3. Why does Jeannette choose to title the book *The Glass Castle* even though the structure is never built?

   The glass castle characterizes Rex Walls' need to create a life of fantasy and adventure for his family in the absence of stability and practicality. Its construction is consistently delayed in the work, but that which it represents endures. Jeannette's memoir is, in part, an erection of this fabled structure. In writing, she takes one step towards fulfilling her father's promise.

4. Explain the role of nature and the attitudes taken toward it in the memoir?

   Without the amenities of modern life, the Walls family is frequently in awe of the beauty of nature. Especially while living in the Midwest, nature becomes a sort of home for the Walls. Rose Mary Walls also instills within her children an appreciation for animals and nature by refusing to kill or harm it with modern technology.

5. What about Jeannette's experience is atypical of general ideas about American poverty? Why do you think Jeannette includes these examples?

   For much of the work, Jeannette and her family live in conditions characteristic of poverty. However, Jeannette's experience also includes rigorous homeschooling from her parents and exposure to classic literature. Despite her conditions, she and her siblings are often placed in the gifted classes in school. In showing that her parents, though poor, were not unintelligent, Jeannette proposes an often undetailed view of America's impoverished.

6. Discuss the role of setting in the novel? How does the theme of the work change when the setting changes?

   Setting is clearly an important part of the work. Indeed, two sections of the novel are named after a particular environment. In addition, there is a clear shift in tone and plot when the Walls move from the desert to Welch, Virginia. Setting not only affects how the family must live but it also influences their hope for escaping poverty.

7. Compare Jeannette's relationship with Brian and Lori to that between her and Maureen. Why are there differences?

Jeannette and her siblings depend on each other for survival. Jeannette and Brian pair together when faced by bullies from outside. Although Lori and Brian differ from Jeannette in their early loss of hope in Rex. Maureen exists as a sort of "black sheep" in the family. Not only does she not have red hair, but she seldom spends time with the family and instead relies on others to care for her. For this reason, Jeannette considers Maureen in need of more protection than the rest of her siblings.

8. Describe the structure of the memoir. Why does Walls decide to frame her story with her adulthood before reflecting on her childhood?

Jeannette begins her story by describing her motivation for writing it. Her mother's urgings that she not hide from her past anymore prompt Jeannette to begin telling her story. Because shame once inhibited her from sharing her story, she begins by describing that which gave her the courage to write it down.

9. Discuss Rose Mary Walls' role as a mother.

Rose Mary Walls commonly seems focused on her aims alone. She loses or quits jobs in order to pursue her profitless career as an artist even at times when her family needs her salary for basic necessities. At times, Rose Mary behaves more like a child than her children, throwing tantrums, refusing to go to work, and creating excuses.

10. Rex Walls frequently makes up fantastical stories to create a life of excitement out of his circumstances. Is this deceitful? In what ways can these stories be seen as an attempt to shield the family from the truth?

Rex Walls tends to create fantastical explanations to keep his children from considering themselves lesser than others because of their lack of money. When the children are young, this seems harmless. He gives them stars for Christmas instead of gifts and makes life an adventure by telling them they are being chased. However, as the children grow older, Rex's stories are used as a means to protect or excuse his behavior instead of as a means to shield his children from the reality of their condition.

# The Walls Family Travels

This map traces the journey of the members of the Walls family across America, over the course of the memoir.

# Author of ClassicNote and Sources

Andrea Clay, author of ClassicNote. Completed on January 17, 2011, copyright held by GradeSaver.

Updated and revised Elizabeth Weinbloom March 31, 2011. Copyright held by GradeSaver.

Jeannette Walls. The Glass Castle. New York: Scribner, 2005.

M&C News. "Pitt's Plan B inks deal with Paramount." Monstersandcritics.com. 2005-06-23. 2011-01-31.
<http://www.monstersandcritics.com/movies/news/printer_8949.php>.

Carol Brennan. "Jeannette Walls." Encyclopedia of World Biography. 2011-01-01. 2011-01-17.
<http://www.notablebiographies.com/newsmakers2/2006-Ra-Z/Walls-Jeannette.html>.

Francine Prose. "'The Glass Castle':Outrageous Misfortune." New York Times. 2005-03-13. 2011-01-17.
<http://www.nytimes.com/2005/03/13/books/review/013COVERPROSE.html>.

Cindy. "Jeannette Walls, The Glass Castle." Conversations with Famous Writers. 2005-10-27. 2011-01-19.
<http://conversationsfamouswriters.blogspot.com/2005/10/jeannette-walls-glass-castle.html>.

Walls, Jeannette. "Truth and Consequences." *Publishers Weekly* 252.37 (2005): 74. *MLA International Bibliography*. EBSCO. Web. 31 Jan. 2011.

# Quiz 1

1. **Where does Jeannette see her mother at the beginning of the work?**
   A. At a party
   B. Rummaging through a dumpster
   C. At a chinese restaurant
   D. At a family reunion

2. **What doll does Jeannette accidentally burn?**
   A. G.I. Joe
   B. Tinkerbell
   C. Don Quixote
   D. Barbie

3. **What is Jeannette's first memory?**
   A. Sleeping beneath the stars
   B. Playing with matches.
   C. Being set on fire.
   D. Eating chewing gum

4. **Why does Maureen get arrested?**
   A. She stabs her mother
   B. For drug abuse
   C. For Stealing clothing from the department store
   D. She is caught drinking alcohol in public

5. **What are the names of Jeannette's three sisters?**
   A. Rose Mary, Dinitia, Clare
   B. Lori, Maureen, and Mary Charlene
   C. Maureen, Lily, Ruth
   D. Briana, Lori, Maureen

6. **What does Jeannette request for her tenth birthday?**
   A. That her father stop drinking.
   B. A stand for her rock collection.
   C. A barbie doll.
   D. A new bicycle.

7. **What two addictions does Rex Walls suffer from**
    A. Gambling and Alcohol
    B. Painkillers and Sugar
    C. Cigarettes and Reading
    D. Excitement and Science

8. **What does Rose Mary want to do for a living?**
    A. Travel
    B. Sell Real Estate
    C. Be an Artist
    D. Teach

9. **What does Rex take his children to the zoo to do?**
    A. Free the animals
    B. See the flamingos
    C. Set fire to a security car
    D. Pet a Cheetah

10. **What does Jeannette try for the first time in the hospital?**
    A. A Blow Dryer
    B. Chewing Gum
    C. Rice Pudding
    D. Crossword Puzzles

11. **How does Jeannette cover up the holes in her pants?**
    A. She wears two pairs of pants at once
    B. She patches them up with extra fabric
    C. She staples the holes together
    D. She colors her skin in with marker

12. **How Does Jeannette increase sales of the school newspaper?**
    A. She lowers the price
    B. She creates a buy one get one free promotion
    C. She adds a gossip column into the newspaper
    D. She includes a birthday column

13. **When does Jeannette move to New York**
   A. After her junior year of high school
   B. After she graduates from high school
   C. When she is 3
   D. When Maureen is born

14. **Why is Dinitia arrested?**
   A. She stabs her mother's boyfriend to death
   B. She lights her house on fire
   C. She steals from the Pub
   D. She beats up Brian and Jeannette

15. **What is Rex always promising to build for his family to live in?**
   A. A new car
   B. A stucco mansion
   C. A house on the riverside
   D. A Glass Castle

16. **What is Rex's nickname for Jeannette**
   A. Mountain Goat
   B. Jeannie
   C. Little Darling
   D. Hillbilly

17. **Jeannette attends _____ College.**
   A. Barnard
   B. Harvard
   C. New York
   D. Baltimore

18. **What happens to the money the Walls children save in Oz, the piggy bank?**
   A. The bill collectors repossess it
   B. Rose Mary spends it on art supplies.
   C. They use it to go to New York
   D. Rex steals it.

## 19. What is the name of Jeannette's first husband.
A. Rex
B. Eric
C. John
D. Marc

## 20. Who is the Black girl Jeannettte befriends in Welch?
A. Taylor
B. LaTasha
C. Dinitia
D. Monique

## 21. Where does Jeannette learn to swim?
A. the ocean
B. An integrated community pool
C. The Hot Pot
D. the bathtub

## 22. What does Lori decide she wants to do as a career?
A. Join the Police force
B. Be a lawyer
C. Be an Artist
D. Teach

## 23. Which hero of Rex's visits Welch?
A. Michael Jackson
B. Elton John
C. Paul Newman
D. Chuck Yeager

## 24. What is the Green Lantern?
A. A pet of Brian's
B. The name of one of the Walls' cars
C. A house of prostitution
D. A flashlight

25. **What type of restaurant does Lori work at in New York?**
   A. A burger joint
   B. A Chinese restaurant
   C. A seafood restaurant
   D. A German restaurant.

# Quiz 1 Answer Key

1. **(B)** Rummaging through a dumpster
2. **(B)** Tinkerbell
3. **(C)** Being set on fire.
4. **(A)** She stabs her mother
5. **(B)** Lori, Maureen, and Mary Charlene
6. **(A)** That her father stop drinking.
7. **(A)** Gambling and Alcohol
8. **(C)** Be an Artist
9. **(D)** Pet a Cheetah
10. **(B)** Chewing Gum
11. **(D)** She colors her skin in with marker
12. **(D)** She includes a birthday column
13. **(A)** After her junior year of high school
14. **(A)** She stabs her mother's boyfriend to death
15. **(D)** A Glass Castle
16. **(A)** Mountain Goat
17. **(A)** Barnard
18. **(D)** Rex steals it.
19. **(B)** Eric
20. **(C)** Dinitia
21. **(C)** The Hot Pot
22. **(C)** Be an Artist
23. **(D)** Chuck Yeager
24. **(C)** A house of prostitution
25. **(D)** A German restaurant.

# Quiz 2

1. **What happens to Erma and Ted's house?**
   A. It is converted into a nursing home
   B. Rex inherits it
   C. The government repossesses it
   D. It burns down

2. **What type of plant is Rose Mary fascinated by in the desert?**
   A. A crooked joshua tree
   B. An upside down cactus
   C. A bushel of Roses
   D. A cave made of sand

3. **What does Ernie Goad call the Walls family when he teases Brian and Jeannette?**
   A. Drunks
   B. Gentle people
   C. Garbage
   D. White trash

4. **What is the name of the newspaper Jeannette first works for in New York City?**
   A. The Chancellor
   B. The New York Times
   C. The Phoenix
   D. Eating Healthy in New York

5. **What illness does Rex contract in New York City?**
   A. Tuberculosis
   B. HIV
   C. A rare tropical disease
   D. Mono

6. **Where does Maureen move to?**
   A. Kansas
   B. Mexico
   C. West Virginia
   D. California

7. **What does Jeannette steal from the jewelry shop?**
    A. A watch
    B. A diamond ring
    C. A pearl necklace
    D. Cuff links for her father

8. **What is the name of the tool Rex plans to build to find gold?**
    A. The Prospector
    B. Rex Walls' Greatest Invention
    C. The Goldenrod 2000
    D. The Sifter

9. **What does Rose Mary ask Jeannette for after Uncle Jim dies?**
    A. $1 Million dollars to buy back his land
    B. a new easel
    C. a down payment for an apartment
    D. electrolysis treatment

10. **Where does Jeannette meet her mother after passing by her at the dumpster?**
    A. At Lori's house
    B. A chinese restaurant
    C. California
    D. At the party

11. **What word does John use to describe Jeannette's scar?**
    A. Gruesome
    B. Textured
    C. Beautiful
    D. Interesting

12. **What does Rex call the act of moving out of a place quickly and stealthily?**
    A. The skedaddle
    B. Eagle Out
    C. The Hustle
    D. Code 401

13. **What sorts of towns do the Walls typically settle in?**
    A. Metropolitan Cities
    B. Tourist areas
    C. Ghost towns
    D. Mining towns

14. **What are Rex's religious views?**
    A. Jewish
    B. Atheist
    C. Agnostic
    D. Southern Baptist

15. **What are Mary Ann's Religious Views?**
    A. Atheist
    B. Catholic
    C. Buddhist
    D. Protestant

16. **What does Jeannette begin to think is a recurring element in her life?**
    A. The Cold
    B. Poverty
    C. Bullying
    D. Fire

17. **What are Jeannette's favorite things to collect?**
    A. Buttons
    B. Fool's Gold
    C. Comic Books
    D. Geodes

18. **How does JuJu die?**
    A. She is hit by a car
    B. Rattlesnake Bite
    C. Poisoning
    D. Old age

19. **What "star" does Jeannette pick out for a Christmas present?**
    A. The North Star
    B. Venus
    C. The Big Dipper
    D. The Sun

20. **How long does Rose Mary claim to have been pregnant with Lori?**
    A. 9 months
    B. 14 months.
    C. 2 weeks
    D. 2 years

21. **What does Jeannette think LBJ stands for at first?**
    A. Lori, Brian, Jeannette
    B. Low Budget Juice
    C. Lyndon B. Johnson
    D. Little Baby Jesus

22. **Who is Maureen named after?**
    A. A famous painter
    B. Her Mother
    C. An actress
    D. Her Grandmothers

23. **What was the house in Battle Mountain formerly used as?**
    A. A shopping mall
    B. A nursey school
    C. A railroad depot
    D. A convenient store

24. **How do Brian and Jeannette get too close to the boundary between turbulence and order?**
    A. They accidentally set a shed on fire while they are inside of it
    B. They get into a fight with a classmate.
    C. They swim in the hot pot without supervision.
    D. They steal from a neighbor.

25. **What happens when Brian is caught stealing pickles from a neighbor?**
    A. His father yells at him
    B. He has to work to pay the neighbor back
    C. He shares the pickles with his family
    D. He is forced to eat them all at once

# Quiz 2 Answer Key

1. **(D)** It burns down
2. **(A)** A crooked joshua tree
3. **(C)** Garbage
4. **(C)** The Phoenix
5. **(A)** Tuberculosis
6. **(D)** California
7. **(A)** A watch
8. **(A)** The Prospector
9. **(A)** $1 Million dollars to buy back his land
10. **(B)** A chinese restaurant
11. **(B)** Textured
12. **(A)** The skedaddle
13. **(D)** Mining towns
14. **(B)** Atheist
15. **(B)** Catholic
16. **(D)** Fire
17. **(D)** Geodes
18. **(B)** Rattlesnake Bite
19. **(B)** Venus
20. **(B)** 14 months.
21. **(A)** Lori, Brian, Jeannette
22. **(D)** Her Grandmothers
23. **(C)** A railroad depot
24. **(A)** They accidentally set a shed on fire while they are inside of it
25. **(D)** He is forced to eat them all at once

# Quiz 3

1. **What does Rex force Brian to give to Ginger, the woman from the Green Lantern?**
   A. A hug
   B. A Sad Sack comic book
   C. Money
   D. His sandwich

2. **What does Billy Deel give to Jeannette as a gift?**
   A. A necklace
   B. A turquoise ring.
   C. A miniature glass castle
   D. A new bicycle

3. **What does Grandma Smith die from?**
   A. Leukemia
   B. Pneumonia
   C. Old age
   D. Breast Cancer

4. **What does the school nurse prescribe for Lori?**
   A. Anxiety Pills
   B. Acne Cream
   C. Anti-Depressants
   D. A pair of eyeglasses.

5. **At the end of the memoir the family gathers to celebrate what holiday?**
   A. Easter
   B. Thanksgiving
   C. Christmas
   D. The 4th of July

6. **How does Rex ruin Christmas?**
   A. He yells at everyone.
   B. He steals all the money for presents.
   C. He burns down the Christmas tree
   D. He criticizes Rose Mary's cooking.

7. **What does Rex suffer just before his death?**
   A. A heart attack.
   B. A stroke
   C. A seizure
   D. An aneurysm

8. **At the end of the novel Jeannette feels she has not offered enough of what to Maureen?**
   A. Attention
   B. Protection
   C. Money
   D. Trust

9. **Jeannette finds her life is similar to a character's in what book?**
   A. A Tree Grows in Brooklyn
   B. Cinderella
   C. Pride and Prejudice
   D. Oliver Twist

10. **How much does Jeannette suspect her mother's land in Texas is worth?**
    A. Practically nothing
    B. 1 million dollars
    C. 8 thousand dollar
    D. 10 million dollars

11. **Dinitia befriends Jeannette after what happens?**
    A. Jeannette rescues a young black boy
    B. They play on the same basketball team
    C. Jeannette moves to a new school
    D. Dinitia protects Jeannette from a bully

12. **What is the suspected cause of Erma's death?**
    A. Alcoholism
    B. Depression
    C. Starvation
    D. Cigarettes

13. **What happens to the foundation of the Glass Castle?**
    A. Rex builds a shed over it
    B. It is filled with garbage
    C. A family of kittens begins living in it
    D. It is flooded

14. **To what type of school does Lori want to apply?**
    A. Business School
    B. Art School
    C. Law school
    D. Cosmetology School

15. **What happens to the ring Jeannette and Brian find in the backyard in Welch?**
    A. They re-bury it
    B. They Pawn it off
    C. Rose Mary uses it to replace her wedding ring
    D. Rex steals it

16. **What does Jeannette ask her mother to do so the family can qualify for welfare?**
    A. Leave Rex
    B. Have another baby
    C. Quit her job
    D. Hide the food in the refrigerator

17. **After the child-welfare officer visits, Jeannette fears _____ ?**
    A. That the officer wants to kidnap her.
    B. That she and her siblings will be separated.
    C. That she will be disowned
    D. That her parents will get into trouble.

18. **What is the name of the school newspaper for which Jeannette writes?**
    A. The Maroon Wave
    B. The Crimson Beach
    C. High School Daily
    D. The Journal

19. **When Lori returns from camp she is determined to do what?**
    A. Have children
    B. Leave Welch
    C. Get married
    D. Be a camp counselor

20. **What does Rex name the Cadillac Coupe DeVille?**
    A. Lady Luck
    B. Big C
    C. Caddy
    D. Elvis

21. **Rex destroys Lori's bust of what famous playwright?**
    A. Moliere
    B. Samuel Beckett
    C. Shakespeare
    D. Tennessee Williams

22. **What des Rex give Jeannette as a parting gift when she leaves Welch?**
    A. His watch
    B. His favorite jackknife
    C. A book of memories
    D. A miniature glass castle

23. **Who is the author of I[The Glass Castle]?**
    A. C.S. Lewis
    B. Rose Mary Walls
    C. Jeannette Walls
    D. Alice Walker

24. **Lori and Brian find a dumpster full of _____?**
    A. Chocolate
    B. Umbrellas
    C. Toys
    D. Money

25. **Billy Deel attacks the Walls children with what?**
    A. His Fists
    B. A bat
    C. A BB Gun
    D. Pepper Spray

# Quiz 3 Answer Key

1. **(B)** A Sad Sack comic book
2. **(B)** A turquoise ring.
3. **(A)** Leukemia
4. **(D)** A pair of eyeglasses.
5. **(B)** Thanksgiving
6. **(C)** He burns down the Christmas tree
7. **(A)** A heart attack.
8. **(B)** Protection
9. **(A)** A Tree Grows in Brooklyn
10. **(B)** 1 million dollars
11. **(A)** Jeannette rescues a young black boy
12. **(A)** Alcoholism
13. **(B)** It is filled with garbage
14. **(B)** Art School
15. **(C)** Rose Mary uses it to replace her wedding ring
16. **(A)** Leave Rex
17. **(B)** That she and her siblings will be separated.
18. **(A)** The Maroon Wave
19. **(B)** Leave Welch
20. **(D)** Elvis
21. **(C)** Shakespeare
22. **(B)** His favorite jackknife
23. **(C)** Jeannette Walls
24. **(A)** Chocolate
25. **(C)** A BB Gun

# Quiz 4

1. **Jeannette Walls enters what professional field?**
   A. Fashion Design
   B. Marketing
   C. Journalism
   D. Acting

2. **As a teacher, Rose Mary has the most trouble with what?**
   A. Grading Homework
   B. Showing up on time
   C. Discipline
   D. Remembering the Material

3. **What does Jeannette collect while living in Battle Mountain?**
   A. Stamps
   B. Barbie Dolls
   C. Coins
   D. Rocks

4. **Brian refuses to wave to _____ from the Green Lantern?**
   A. Ginger
   B. Maureen
   C. Baby Face
   D. Jeannette

5. **All of the Walls children have red hair except who?**
   A. Maureen
   B. Jeannette
   C. Lori
   D. Brian

6. **Who is the youngest of the Walls children?**
   A. Maureen
   B. Jeannette
   C. Lori
   D. Brian

7. **Who is the eldest Walls child?**
   A. Maureen
   B. Jeannette
   C. Lori
   D. Brian

8. **What type of surgery does Jeanette receive?**
   A. Plastic surgery
   B. Skin Graft
   C. Bone fusion
   D. Brain

9. **What do the neighbors do when they overhear Rose Mary and Rex fighting in Battle Mountain?**
   A. They intervene
   B. They watch from outside
   C. They tell them to be quiet
   D. They call the police

10. **The Walls children are placed in gifted classes in every town but _____?**
    A. Blithe
    B. Phoenix
    C. Battle Mountain
    D. Welch

11. **The Walls children travel to Battle Mountain in the back of what type of vehicle?**
    A. A Cadillac
    B. A Boat
    C. A U-Haul
    D. A Plane

12. **When Lori is stung by a scorpion where do her parents take her for treatment?**
    A. The Witch doctor
    B. Rose Mary's mother's house
    C. The Dermatologist
    D. The hospital

13. **What does Billy Deel show Jeannette at his home?**
    A. His Drunk and Sleeping Father
    B. A new toy
    C. A turquoise ring
    D. How to do calculus

14. **During an argument, Rex throws what of Rose Mary's out of the window?**
    A. Canvas
    B. Favorite Vase
    C. Paint brushes
    D. Wedding Ring

15. **How many times is Jeannette married?**
    A. Once
    B. Three Times
    C. Twice
    D. Never

16. **What does Rex give his children one Christmas?**
    A. A puppy
    B. Matching baseball caps
    C. Money
    D. Stars

17. **How old is Jeannette when she is first burned?**
    A. 3
    B. 13
    C. 16
    D. 26

18. **What denomination are many of Maureen's friends in Welch?**
    A. Baptist
    B. Catholic
    C. Protestant
    D. Pentecostal

## 19. Brian seldom does what?

A. Curses

B. Listens

C. Acts out

D. Cries

## 20. How does Rose Mary get to her teaching job in Welch?

A. A Carpool

B. She Walks

C. She Drives

D. She sleeps in the school

## 21. Jeannette makes extra money doing all but the following?

A. Selling Rocks

B. Selling Custom-made Posters

C. Starting a Lemonade Stand

D. Babysitting

## 22. Why doesn't Jeannette go to Columbia University?

A. It doesn't have a good journalism program

B. She doesn't want to live in NYC

C. They don't enroll women

D. It costs too much money

## 23. When is I[The Glass Castle] published?

A. 1964

B. 1989

C. 2005

D. 2011

## 24. What is not a major theme of I[The Glass Castle]?

A. Racism

B. Poverty

C. Fantasy and Imagination

D. Alcoholism

## 25. What type of work is I[The Glass Castle]?
   A. A memoir
   B. A work of fiction
   C. A play
   D. An editorial

# Quiz 4 Answer Key

1. **(C)** Journalism
2. **(C)** Discipline
3. **(D)** Rocks
4. **(A)** Ginger
5. **(A)** Maureen
6. **(A)** Maureen
7. **(C)** Lori
8. **(B)** Skin Graft
9. **(B)** They watch from outside
10. **(D)** Welch
11. **(C)** A U-Haul
12. **(A)** The Witch doctor
13. **(A)** His Drunk and Sleeping Father
14. **(A)** Canvas
15. **(C)** Twice
16. **(D)** Stars
17. **(A)** 3
18. **(D)** Pentecostal
19. **(D)** Cries
20. **(A)** A Carpool
21. **(C)** Starting a Lemonade Stand
22. **(C)** They don't enroll women
23. **(C)** 2005
24. **(A)** Racism
25. **(A)** A memoir

# ClassicNotes

# GradeSaver™

*Getting you the grade since 1999*™

## Other ClassicNotes from GradeSaver™

1984
Absalom, Absalom
Adam Bcdc
The Adventures of Augie
    March
The Adventures of
    Huckleberry Finn
The Adventures of Tom
    Sawyer
The Aeneid
Agamemnon
The Age of Innocence
The Alchemist (Coelho)
The Alchemist (Jonson)
Alice in Wonderland
All My Sons
All Quiet on the Western
    Front
All the King's Men
All the Pretty Horses
Allen Ginsberg's Poetry
The Ambassadors
American Beauty
And Then There Were
    None
Angela's Ashes
Animal Farm
Anna Karenina
Anthem
Antigone
Antony and Cleopatra
Aristotle's Ethics
Aristotle's Poetics
Aristotle's Politics
As I Lay Dying
As You Like It

Astrophil and Stella
Atlas Shrugged
Atonement
The Awakening
Babbitt
The Bacchae
Bartleby the Scrivener
The Bean Trees
The Bell Jar
Beloved
Benito Cereno
Beowulf
Bhagavad-Gita
Billy Budd
Black Boy
Bleak House
Bless Me, Ultima
Blindness
The Bloody Chamber
Bluest Eye
The Bonfire of the
    Vanities
The Book of the Duchess
    and Other Poems
The Book Thief
Brave New World
Breakfast at Tiffany's
Breakfast of Champions
The Brief Wondrous Life
    of Oscar Wao
The Brothers Karamazov
The Burning Plain and
    Other Stories
A Burnt-Out Case
By Night in Chile
Call of the Wild

Candide
The Canterbury Tales
Cat on a Hot Tin Roof
Cat's Cradle
Catch-22
The Catcher in the Rye
The Caucasian Chalk
    Circle
Charlotte's Web
The Cherry Orchard
The Chocolate War
The Chosen
A Christmas Carol
Christopher Marlowe's
    Poems
Chronicle of a Death
    Foretold
Civil Disobedience
Civilization and Its
    Discontents
A Clockwork Orange
The Color of Water
The Color Purple
Comedy of Errors
Communist Manifesto
A Confederacy of
    Dunces
Confessions
Connecticut Yankee in
    King Arthur's Court
The Consolation of
    Philosophy
Coriolanus
The Count of Monte
    Cristo
The Country Wife

For our full list of over 250 Study Guides, Quizzes,
Sample College Application Essays, Literature Essays and E-texts, visit:

**www.gradesaver.com**

# ClassicNotes

# GradeSaver™

## *Getting you the grade since 1999*™

# ClassicNotes

# GradeSaver™

*Getting you the grade since 1999*™

## Other ClassicNotes from GradeSaver™

In Our Time
In the Time of the
    Butterflies
Inherit the Wind
An Inspector Calls
Into the Wild
Invisible Man
The Island of Dr. Moreau
Jane Eyre
Jazz
The Jew of Malta
Joseph Andrews
The Joy Luck Club
Julius Caesar
The Jungle
Jungle of Cities
Kama Sutra
Kate Chopin's Short
    Stories
Kidnapped
King Lear
The Kite Runner
Last of the Mohicans
Leaves of Grass
The Legend of Sleepy
    Hollow
Leviathan
Libation Bearers
Life is Beautiful
Life of Pi
Light In August
The Lion, the Witch and
    the Wardrobe
Little Women
Lolita

Long Day's Journey Into
    Night
Look Back in Anger
Lord Jim
Lord of the Flies
The Lord of the Rings:
    The Fellowship of the
    Ring
The Lord of the Rings:
    The Return of the
    King
The Lord of the Rings:
    The Two Towers
A Lost Lady
The Lottery and Other
    Stories
Love in the Time of
    Cholera
The Love Song of J.
    Alfred Prufrock
The Lovely Bones
Lucy
Macbeth
Madame Bovary
Maggie: A Girl of the
    Streets and Other
    Stories
Manhattan Transfer
Mankind: Medieval
    Morality Plays
Mansfield Park
The Marrow of Tradition
The Master and
    Margarita
MAUS

The Mayor of
    Casterbridge
Measure for Measure
Medea
Merchant of Venice
Metamorphoses
The Metamorphosis
Middlemarch
A Midsummer Night's
    Dream
Moby Dick
A Modest Proposal and
    Other Satires
Moll Flanders
Mother Courage and Her
    Children
Mrs. Dalloway
Much Ado About
    Nothing
My Antonia
Mythology
Native Son
Nickel and Dimed: On
    (Not) Getting By in
    America
Night
Nine Stories
No Exit
Northanger Abbey
Notes from Underground
O Pioneers
The Odyssey
Oedipus Rex or Oedipus
    the King
Of Mice and Men
The Old Man and the Sea

For our full list of over 250 Study Guides, Quizzes,
Sample College Application Essays, Literature Essays and E-texts, visit:

**www.gradesaver.com**

# ClassicNotes

## Gr垪deSaver™

*Getting you the grade since 1999*™

## Other ClassicNotes from GradeSaver™

The Spanish Tragedy
Spenser's Amoretti and
    Epithalamion
Spring Awakening
The Stranger
A Streetcar Named
    Desire
Sula
The Sun Also Rises
Tale of Two Cities
The Taming of the Shrew
The Tempest
Tender is the Night
Tess of the D'Urbervilles
Their Eyes Were
    Watching God
Things Fall Apart
The Things They Carried
A Thousand Splendid
    Suns
The Threepenny Opera
Through the Looking
    Glass
Thus Spoke Zarathustra
The Time Machine
Titus Andronicus
To Build a Fire
To Kill a Mockingbird
To the Lighthouse
The Tortilla Curtain
Treasure Island
Trifles
Troilus and Cressida
Tropic of Cancer
Tropic of Capricorn
Tuesdays With Morrie

The Turn of the Screw
Twelfth Night
Twilight
Ulysses
Uncle Tom's Cabin
Utopia
Vanity Fair
A Very Old Man With
    Enormous Wings
Villette
The Visit
Volpone
Waiting for Godot
Waiting for Lefty
Walden
Washington Square
The Waste Land
Where the Red Fern
    Grows
White Fang
White Noise
White Teeth
Who's Afraid of Virginia
    Woolf
Wide Sargasso Sea
Winesburg, Ohio
The Winter's Tale
The Woman Warrior
Wordsworth's Poetical
    Works
Woyzeck
A Wrinkle in Time
Wuthering Heights
The Yellow Wallpaper
Yonnondio: From the
    Thirties

For our full list of over 250 Study Guides, Quizzes,
Sample College Application Essays, Literature Essays and E-texts, visit:

**www.gradesaver.com**

Made in the USA
San Bernardino, CA
03 May 2018